Heresies

Orlando Ricardo Menes

POEMS

UNIVERSITY OF NEW MEXICO PRESS † ALBUQUERQUE

© 2015 by Orlando Ricardo Menes
All rights reserved. Published 2015
Printed in the United States of America
20 19 18 17 16 15   1 2 3 4 5 6

Library of Congress Cataloging-in-Publication Data
Menes, Orlando Ricardo.
 [Poems. Selections]
 Heresies : poems / Orlando Ricardo Menes.
    pages ; cm. — (Mary Burritt Christiansen Poetry Series)
 ISBN 978-0-8263-3521-0 (softcover : acid-free paper) — ISBN 978-0-8263-3522-7 (electronic)
 I. Title.
 PS3563.E52A6 2015
 811'.54—dc23
                            2014049530

Cover illustration courtesy of Photobucket
Author photo courtesy of Michael Wiens at the University of Notre Dame
Cover designed by Felicia Cedillos
Composed in Dante MT 11.5/13.5
Display font is Fairfield LT

for my wife, Ivis, and our two children, Valerie and Adrian

Contents

St. Rustica, Patroness of Tobacco Growers

for Severo Sarduy

When macaws squawk the Angelus
fields of *marabú* smolder through veils
of passion vine, hills slashed, burned

for growing *tabaco de sal*, island strain
that blooms in salt air, spume-drift, brackish drizzle
of Lenten days. The burly saint plows high cliffs,

shark's-tooth ridges, alluvial slopes plunging
down tidal reefs, cuttlefish lagoons. Old, bony,
barnacled with sores, oxen list to the wind

as they pull a carrack's rudder, black ironwood,
cleaving fish-meal soil, seaweed mulch, pelican guano.
Saints Edith and Clare, twenty other virgins—

spry, long-legged as egrets—sow the tiny
seeds, forty thousand to an ounce; thumbs wet
with earth count cowries, periwinkle shells,

rosaries to la Vírgen—Mother of Carib Waters—
whose fog fumigates saplings (pests: slug, louse,
budworm, moth caterpillar, cricket nymph,

weevil larva), whose dew repels the dread
mosaic, whose mist gauzes culled leaves in chapels
of wild cane leeward to the sun. Sweated, dried,

cured in one hundred days, rolled on stone altars,
pressed between hardwood missals, banded with palm-leaf
Hail Marys, *el tabaco* is smoked at prayer,

Mass, all holy days, especially Our Lady's fiesta
when they gather at daybreak in a grotto beneath the sea,
her image carved from shell-encrusted ebony,

1

shark's-skin face, cockle eyes, tight braids of green leaf,
sea-grape blossoms. They celebrate her coronation,
music of conch, pink-coral organelles, singing Magnificats,

Salve Reginas, Ave Marias from leaf-bound hymnals,
pausing to partake of *tabaco*, hold their breaths as they inhale
throat-burning *bronco*, exhale alleluias, cough so hard

eyes run. As plumes rise through the grotto's oculus,
St. Rustica puffs on a corona, preaches the plant's sacrament,
whose raw juice healed lepers, made Jericho's blind see again,

whose smoke transported Elijah to the throned God who has
no name, whose tender shoots swaddled Baby Jesus,
whose brittle brown leaves were Christ's cerements.

Middle Passage

for Alejo Carpentier

A litany of galleons—breakwater—
crusted with oyster mandorlas, limpet medals,
a carrack's mast that flies shrouds
of martyrs, racked riggings, sins' ballast.

Nuns in pirogues charge a slaver's sloop,
volley crucifixes, maledict in Yoruba,
swerve into reefs where corals consecrate
the iron chains of drowned slaves,

then back to port the nuns snag orphans
who glide the swells in sargasso blankets,
turtle-shell skiffs, cuddled by dolphins,
brooded by cormorants as they cast ashore

to Mercy's island—Our Lady's archipelago—
where stowaway seeds, vagrant birds,
the innocents of wrecked slavers find refuge
in sugarloaf coves, marzipan sands,

molasses marshes where the sacred ibis
plods for gastropods, a roost of bulbuls
chattering hymns high in the baobabs,
the nuns' hothouse of *Musa paradisiaca*

whose nectarous paps infants suckle
until weaned by mashed cocoyams,
green plantain *fufu*, and okra stews—
their abbey at the mouth of Río Oshún

a nave of kapok trees, royal-palm spires,
banyan buttresses, an altar of green
fishtail fronds, Ficus twigs, coconut water
in calabash stoups where novices carve

madonnas in ebony, cowrie eyes, gowns
of goat hide, sea urchin crowns, a gang
of nuns that chops the spirit trees, bullock carts
carrying the bloody logs to seaside sheds

where they saw, plane, and peg tiny caravels—
dreadlock ropes, rood masts, lambskin sails,
Our Lady's red-coral throne garlanded
with jellyfish tentacles, stingray barbs, hex bombs

(bones, sticks, herbs) in each bow—a flotilla
of black Marías to cross the Middle Passage
on vestal currents, reclaim every slave port,
Ivory Coast to Angola, Ouidah, Kikombo.

St. Lazarus the African Instructs Those Who Seek His Healing

for Kamau Brathwaite

Banish from your minds that old, white leper on crutches you see
engraved in paper or baked into porcelain. I am ebony, eyes & mouth
snail shells, my soul the pungent charcoal of Accra. Be generous
when I come to beg at your church, your house, your crossroads.
Deny me alms & my crutch is a bonebreaker, my spit a missile
of virulence. But just as I make you sick I can make you well. My
wounds are wells of elixir, my teardrops salves, my skin ampuled
with vaccines. I ask for little in return. Big cigars, aged rum, white
doves. When you pray to me wear sackcloth, chain one ankle to an
anvil, then slither on your back. Chant my names with drums &
gourds. Babalú Boku. Babalú Beluja. Babalú Oloko. Never forget
Calabar, blacks' Calvary. So many cargoed to sugar islands, silver
mines, cotton fields, just rawhide to chew, sweat & urine to drink,
whole villages packed tighter than sardines. Where was Jesus to raise
the dead in those coffins with sails? Where was Jesus to whip those
slavers to the bone? Where was Jesus to walk my people home across
the swells? I will not abandon you with paradoxes, false hope, hollow
blessings.

Toussaint L'Ouverture Imprisoned at Fort de Joux

Jura Mountains, France, 1803

Once a generalissimo, I now wear the rags of a cutter, my plantation of snow where trees shiver without leaves, my icy cell where wind cuts like blades of cane, jailers tapping taunts on iron bars, *monkey, monkey in a cage.* Haiti is lost to me, her cities plundered, her forests burnt. Christophe stole my lands. Bonaparte shipped my family to France like sacks of charcoal in the brig. Traitors abound on earth as in Heaven. In times of war trust no one but the gravedigger. Why do you forsake me, Father? Am I not your rightful son, black as the tar of your holy fire? I hate myself for calling my people's faith savage, I the greatest traitor who sold his talismans for a scrawny man nailed to sticks. Forgive me Ogún, loa of war, whose iron sword helped me win battles, I the infidel who prayed to saints. I beseech you now, Lord Ogún. Slay the mulattoes. Miscegenation is treason. Only blacks shall inherit the earth. Your armies of vodun will raze every church, smite every shrine. Wild hogs will feed on hosts. Mother Africa is our holy land. Abomey, our Vatican of idols & sorcery.

Solomon of the Antilles Proposes His New Jerusalem

Hear me castaways of the faith, runaways from dogma, excommunicates.
I bring good news of a New Jerusalem, Carib Sea. Let us paddle—God's
canoes—to His rosary of cays, barren as vellum for psalms, & build
our temple there without hammer, axe, or saw. Our tools the oblong
stone, the sawfish's snout, the bladed clam, the auger of periwinkle.
Don't fret because there's no hardwood or that the coral quarries are
poor. Cedar logs will wash ashore. Dowels will rain down from thunder
clouds. The wind will not topple our towers of tortoise shell or waves
tear the sharkskin veil. No metal to cast our shrines? Salt pans will dry to
silver ore. Hermit crabs will lay gold nuggets. What will we sacrifice to
Elohim? The barracudas we spear in shallows, the sea cows we corral in
red mangroves, our daily lives ruled by devotionals set to the tides as we
sip fish blood, chew bitter sargassum, our prayers choraled to conchs,
turtle tambourines.

St. Primitivo, Patron of Heretics, Exhorts His Catechumens

Don't pray for favors kneeling on little stones or scribbling pleas that you roll into a scroll. Fate is wind you can't control. How often it kills the candle's flame, blows dirt into hallowed wax. And aren't tapers just dribblers of doubt? Utility is holier than ritual. Put those fonts to good use as bird baths, those missals as mulch, those catafalques as oxcarts. You want to be pious? Hang laundry from the paschal cross. Grow basil in a pyx. Knead dough on the altar. What is incense anyway but smog of piety. The unleavened Host? Just a corpse of starch. Faith demands a primal heart. Tress your hair with spikes & thistles. Scorch your forehead, a diadem of blisters. Dip your hands in lye & smell the dew of Calvary. Sacrifice a spring lamb, hewing meat off the bone with flaked flint, blanching a humerus to carve your chant.

St. Barbara, Patroness of Gunners

Saltpeter is the rock of my church whose cannons blast bombs of beatitude, whose mortars choir the Creed, our martyrs' catacombs of concrete, bar, & mesh steel, a stone bunker to hear Mass for when the infidels shell. How I love the smell of gunpowder as we hymn fusillades of alleluia, ears ringing with canticles, high organ that bellows Aves, serpentine & falconet. In my armory by the Carib Sea, I trill Salvos, high-pitched, to Regina, kiss the pistoled crucifix, 44 calibers of zeal, pull tight my girdle of bullets, light the fuse. I spurn the fine musket of theology. True devotion—a blunderbuss. Only a howitzer can persuade the heretic or the harquebus enforce canon law. God calls me to spread the gospel with shotgun & shrapnel. Catechize with a carbine, He says. Fire culverins to sway the heathens. Don't let Mercy lure you to laxity.

St. Longinus at Calvary

Whoever stripped, whipped, cussed the Son of God, may His blood be on you & all your whelps till Adam rises from the grave. If you spat out lies, may rats nest in your groin as you sleep. If you cast lots, may the Lord's donkey break wind in your face. Beware, you riffraff, defilers of his gallows, I am the warrior who slings leaden olives in the eyes, cudgels so hard that lungs heave like sails, lances the blasphemer like a spring lamb for the spit. Tremble, hooligans, for the earth will soon crack, vines choke the Judas tree, gall fall from Sabbath clouds. Like ducklings in a pond, famine, drought, & plague will follow Death. You will eat seeds dropped by ruminants, drink sour wine, wear the threadbare gown of potter's field. All you brutes who mocked Him as King of the Jews, know that his reign will outlast empire or nation. His fifth wound will outgush Moses' rock. On this skull of a hill above Jerusalem, his flesh-&-bone temple will be eternal unlike Solomon's stone.

St. Giles the Hermit

To abominate buildings is my creed, whether house, church, or
granary. Thatching wastes fodder. Glass atrophies sunlight. And what
is lumber but a butchered tree? God demands altars of unhewn stone,
culled from the ground, never quarried. Shame on the mason who
gelds the granite, the sawyer who cleaves the slate. God commands
us to live among the rocks, especially the humble limestone, brittle
& porous like faith itself. How homely the outcrop on a windy sea
cliff, the old sinkhole shaded by banyan trees, the lair of debris after
a landslide. Green weeds for a bed, a pillow of soft earth, leathery
leaves on which to scratch happy hymns, praying for the day our souls
petrify to everlasting life.

Eschatology

Days of thaw, early spring, the grotto's saints shed
their ice albs, eyes healed of winter's cataracts,
hard-packed haloes dripping into slush.
Next to the scourged maple, a wrought cross
bleeds rust water into my right hand, this gritty
residue that fails to transubstantiate into
Christ's wound (or is it the eye, as Crashaw says),
and thus rust is just rust. At the iron rack,
I light a crooked candle, tin crown, spine of red beads,
and goad the wick with a stick, tease the fire
with whistly breaths, grin as a pilgrim woman scowls,
hushes. Isn't irreverence a sign of holiness?
The virgin taunts her ravisher, the martyr mocks his torturer,
or as St. Lawrence would have said, *Turn me over,*
dunces, and poke those lazy coals. The zealous possess
a deadpan sense of humor, cold irony sacramental,
the belly laugh vulgar perhaps, yet still a portent
of deliverance. If I had my own creed, the Mass
would be a spectacle of gaffes, riddles, puns, tricks,
tongue twisters, even slapstick, the Three Stooges my Trinity,
Chaplin, Keaton, and Cantinflas my prophets, their liturgy
of jokes the surest path to grace in a fallen world.

Siglo de Oro

Mannerists exhumed
the saints from sediments
of sentiment
(an intensity that is almost modern),
fleshed them in acid greens,
acetylene blues,
sulfurous yellows,
bruised reds,
emetic blacks—

as in El Greco's St. Francis
kneeling beside a gnarly brown tree,
his jaw whittled
by too many fasts,
long, gangly fingers
that splay like palm blades
crossed for prayer.

His right eye,
huge as a cherimoya seed,
gazes upon a crucifix,
Christ's sallow body
like saltwater taffy
pulled for Ascension Day
when not just his soul
rose to Heaven

but also those of acolytes
and novices martyred at Easter,
the luckiest day to lose
one's life and be reborn
in the Isthmus of Innocents,
alkaline shallows, carbuncle clouds,
where the blessèd
chant doxologies as they splash,
play volleyball
on a beach of cinders,
cyanic surf of eventide.

St. Mena, Gardener of Metals

for Kwame Dawes

I hallow the lichens that bloom pig iron to ferruginous corallita, bow
to the molds that pit iridium bracts, bless the brume that patinates
glades of serrated brass. In orchards manured with antimony, I
harvest bushels of burnished mangoes, galvanized guavas, nickel-
budded pawpaws, those tin naseberries that soon rot to pewter. And
in my hothouse of mist, a cast-iron canopy, I tend the stray rhodium,
groom the cast-off vanadium, graft the foundling gallium, braze the
misunderstood cerium. Beware you misers of gold, you hoarders of
silver, you ransomers of platinum, you abductors of palladium. I will
crack your vaults, pilfer your strongboxes, then release your captives
to the flame, tossing the molten clots into breakwater sloughs,
floating the slag over dark waters, ploughing the raw bullion into
limestone's watery womb.

St. Solda, Patroness of Welders

I am the apostle of solder, gospel of acetylene & electric arc, my
staff the welding rod, my church of junk found, junk borrowed, junk
bartered, junk bought at flea markets, anything from an eggbeater
to a brass bushing to a truck flywheel. No wooden pietàs, no plaster
Christ Childs, no sandstone saints, but scrap-metal angels with ball-
bearing eyes, windmill wings, pontoon feet. Clad in a bull's-hide
habit, armored wimple, I solder flatware skeletons for the Day of
the Dead, fuse a synod's schisms with flux, sculpt the Corpus Christi
monstrance, a drum brake with fan-blade cross, rake's-teeth rays, my
processional of nuns on rusted stilts, roller-skate altar boys, prosthetic
donkeys. In my grotto of dreck by sacramental smelters, I weld
virgin litanies, 12-gauge beads, scribble magnificats on molten steel,
Epiphany's flame, sparks of Bethlehem.

St. Zita, Patroness of Bakers, Explains the Eucharist

If it were up to me, the Host would be leavened bread, so that
Christ's body is fragrant to the nose, tasty to the tongue—not that
plain wafer deader than bookkeeper's paper. Transubstantiation is
gobbledygook, but I do understand yeast. Not the wild kind that
breeds in cauldrons of dank air; I mean the bloom, that soft, white
powder on black grapes before they get squeezed to must then vinify
in casks of Calvary. My yeast comes from merlots plump as fish eyes I
keep safe from molds in a tin tabernacle, my paschal oven by the altar
stone where I bongo the dough, roll the loaf, three taps on the rump.
Sanctus, sanctus, sanctus. Let it stand half a day tucked in Veronica's
veil. Yeast requires patience & a calm hand. To knead slowly is a
baker's reverence. Sugar, sourdough, & spice make paradise. I bake
cardamom cookies for the Sabbath, marzipan for Mother Mary,
walnut cake for the Last Supper. Even Judas gets a ginger effigy. Yeast
is all you need to raise the dead.

St. Francis Xavier Converts the Vegetarians at Goa

Unlike your blue, peacock-plumed Krishna who faints at the sight
of blood, our Holy Father is no plant-eater or milk-drinker, but a
lover of beef, rare, runny, & on the bone—bullock's shank, steer's
rib, heifer's cheek, oxtail, springer's porterhouse, etc. Don't dillydally
with butter, spices, herbs. God's condiment? Blood, blood, & more
blood. You say it's a sin to eat a cow, better to starve than cook a calf.
But don't ruminants spend all day chewing, farting, mooing? Cull
those lazy cows for the slaughterhouse. Suckle their calves with a
knife. Dress the yearling for those hot hickory coals. Clap, ululate,
stomp. Hew boughs from Brahma bulls & feast till you swell. Slice
sweetbreads for the angels. Fry liver to break a fast, grill hearts in
fellowship. Pleasing God is easy. Even gristle propitiates.

St. Zucchero, Patron of Sugar Mills

O children of the Congo, Niger, Gambia, welcome to my sugar
chapel on this Sunday, day of the drum. Go ahead, beat on the
goatskin, dance with blistered feet. Let your sorrows drain off like
molasses. Drown your worries in golden cachaça. Tomorrow you
will do the Lord's work as scummers, cutters, weeders, ratters,
rollers, boilers, clarifiers, etc. Know that He sees everywhere, hears
the unhearable, forgets nothing. Behold the power of His cane,
stalks like lances, cutlass leaves, snare roots. Serve Him with fear,
obey His overseers, hack the runaway with your reaping blades. To
the righteous Our Lord of the Cane promises soft lashes, caramel
scars, lush wombs. Vex Him & you will suffer Hell's eternal boiling
house. For whites alone Heaven is paradise, but don't agonize. God
loves the hardworking slave. There's a special place, a way station
called Purgatory, where purging houses purify dusky souls (treacles,
muscovados, demeraras) to the whitest clay sugar.

St. Salina, Patroness of Salters

Antillean seas surge at Passiontide,
marimbas plunk daybreak's matin.
And after they slip into habits,
strap on banana wimples, slather bile
of barracuda to repel biting *guasasas*,

St. Salina and her twelve anchorites
—orphans, maroons, castaways—
sing conga canticles as they slog sloughs,
trot marshes, swim to the cloistral
saltworks. On jags of gray oolite,

knobby hands kindle Ficus fires,
boil sloshy brine in cast-iron ciboria
till there's plenty for pickles and cures,
alms to the saltless too, even those
flawless crystals that hallow tart wine

of sea grapes. Then the Saltites feast
not on Easter but on Good Friday
as pinwheels sparkle at every station,
palm-fat candles float in bittern stoups,
altar girls crown Christ with nettles.

Freed from their fast, they gorge
on pickled shark's fetus, manatee fatback,
sea urchin ceviche. Teenage novices
gossip, snort sal volatile in chapel.
Dead crones, beatific, float to Heaven
after brining in clay coffins forty nights.

Then at 3 p.m., hour of the torn veil,
St. Salina climbs the coral altar,
bends slightly, signs the cross, salt-
scoured fingers turn pages of the Brine
Bible, her homily in raspy contralto.

Blessèd is the sea that sours the gall,
that soaks the cerecloth that stings the wound.
O cradle of our covenant, when your waters
bloat our bodies, we pass the stones of sin,
and salted with fire we rise to paradise.

St. Vitus and the Ants

There's no choreography in rapture,
the apostles cannot sing one canticled note,
and St. Vitus is no swooning dancer,
not even a bunioned shuffler, but a dumpy dolt
who clops, clunks, drools whenever
the Holy Spirit tickles his bulbous head.
Like all bumblers, St. Vitus hates wild things,
and though haphazard in his crusade
to extirpate all leafy trees and shrubs,
the hermit never tires or thirsts
as he whacks the ivied hog plum,
rips any oxeye berry that sneaks
onto his domain of dust.
One muggy vesper, St. Vitus slips
while hacking down a copse;
the spun metal cracks a banana tree's spine,
stabbing its blossoming heart.
Fire ants hemorrhage from the wound
and scorch the saint's skin, sear eyes,
blaze ears as he gasps, jolts, douses with dirt.
Ponds boil, brush snaps, seeds pop
as the ants break a path, fast consuming
every thatched hut, plantain grove,
corn hollow. St. Vitus shakes in the mud,
his bloated fingers scratching bites,
yet soon feels giddy from the ants' venom,
howling the *boogaloo*, moaning a mambo
as legs clack like claves and flat feet *bongó*.

St. Dorothy, Patroness of Bartenders

Carouse in my cantina, all you drunkards, louts, good-for-nothings.
Vent your troubles at my altar of hooch. Confess with wine, rugged
riojas & ribeiros. Guzzle shots of faith, drafts of hope, charity's
highball. Why should worship be temperate? Swill, jag, & quaff.
Dance the sambuca, wiggle to grappa. Spread my gospel to the water
drinkers. Catechize with cordials. Muddle mojitos for Mass. Shake
& strain cocktails. To abstain is mortal sin. Beware of teetotalers
who scorn the Eucharist, tempting with grape juice or ginger beer,
heretics who deny that God's clouds rained alcohol, life's water, on
the seventh day. Praise be to His seven spirits: gin, vodka, whiskey,
rum, tequila, brandy, & schnapps. O Mother of God, Vírgen de
Guadalupe, we offer you this Assumption Day no vulgar bloody
marys but tequila blanca, Jerusalem bitters, a garnish of prickly pear.

St. Campesina, Patroness of Water Healers

Holy are the illiterate, the vulgar of tongue. Every written word's
a lie, a blasphemy. Even the Bible tempts with hearsay. Water is the
parchment of angels, & I read their scribbles in purls, riffles, rings, &
eddies, prophecies that sizzle in my ears. Medicines are wicked, warn
the angels, doctors devils, pharmacists dogs, nurses whores. Burn
those balsams, pills, unguents, plugs. Storm hospitals & asylums.
Water alone cures ill thoughts, manias, all infirmities, but don't cup
it in your hands or drink it from a glass. Water stays pure if suckled
from teats of rock, licked off the dewy ferns. I am no sorceress, no
demon's concubine. I break the conjuring sticks, stomp the bone
spells. Pilgrims from all over Cuba flood my valley. I cure the walkers,
squatters, kneelers. The rich & the poor, those black as polish, those
white as cassava. They call me saint, paint my image on cardboard,
carve statues of soap. But I don't charge them a dark cent, refuse to
barter or take a gift. I don't sleep or sit down. I eat the dirt of tobacco
fields. I dream oceans of salve. Holy water gushes from my mouth.

St. Dollar Welcomes Cuban Refugees at the Freedom Tower

I am the seer of financiers, patron of free markets, pardoner to swindlers. Truth is cold cash. Profit beats out charity. The law of supply & demand is my covenant. Scrap love of country, junk all pieties. Your Lady of Charity marches in olive green down the Malecón, your apostle Martí a dummy blathering the communist creed. Homesick? Drink a cuba libre on the beach. Let ripples of nostalgia tickle your feet. Greed is good, money the root of sanctity. Graft a Goodwill, embezzle a telethon. In my haven of laissez-faire, we pray at the till for dividends, swipe away our sins with scapulars of Visa, MasterCard. To cajole some grace, give alms to grifters, adopt a pickpocket, go on pilgrimage to Wall Street. My articles of faith? Fraud, scam, & bribery. The rich leap to Heaven. The poor just loiter in the grave.

St. Cajetan, Patron of Gamblers

Why dawdle with Hail Marys when it's Lady Luck you really seek?
Spin the roulette of rosary beads. Go for broke, picking your numbers
christologically: 5 (wounds), 7 (words), 8 (beatitudes), etc., till his
final 33. Don't ever choose 13 or 30, Judas numbers, sucker bets. Cut,
shuffle, riffle those holy cards made in Italy. Pray hard for the five of
martyrs. Shout hallelujah if it's the five of incorruptibles. Shake those
saints' bones in the chalice. Roll them out hard ways, horn-high, for
that heavenly pair of sixes, three times in a row. Take a chance at jai
alai: trifecta of Father, Son, Holy Spirit. Going through a string of bad
luck? Play the blackjack of virgins, the fiery-crown poker, the deuces
wild Madonna. Trump that god-awful jinx, clinch that good fortune
with gospel bingo, miracles' lottery, jackpots of grace.

Seeds of Stone

Archipelagoes of grace, twilight's *caramelo*, the seraphim trumpet
the Sabbath, & I—Judas—spite the temple, slurp the oyster, sew my
circumcised skin with a cast-off lizard's hide. Let the moon lose its
light. Let the late rains of summer sog grainfields to sows' gristle. Let
dawn rouse the Dead Sea, & I will splash the pungent swells, roam
the knurls & jags, bend down into a crook of rock to wound my
knees, scrape my hands, suck the saltiest of waters, & feel blessed for
gasping, retching. *To doubt is the holy of holies*, the brine angels sing,
& I question the sweetness of rivers that swash sedges at daybreak
or whether faith alone can heave the cold sea to nacreous clouds. I
coax the lean rains of winter, distrust spring downpours, pray for the
drizzle that soaks collops of silt & sprouts to barley seeds of stone.

Bishop Torquemada's Homily for the Poor

Praise be to you who bear burdens with bent backs, your spines like
stones through an iron rod. Who can fault you if slow to flee when
quakes wreck mud houses, storms flood your caves. You hold no
grudge, feel no envy toward those who hoard the firewood trees, the
clean wells, the good land to plow. The poorest among you know that
happiness springs from hardship. How well you mill limestone into
flour, make cheese from tree sap. You are by instinct tame, obedient,
piety the mortar between your bones, your stony feet slogging
through life's thistles & burrs. Don't despair over sins unrepented. An
auto-da-fé well done shaves off a thousand years in Purgatory. Soon
my bells will toll, my stakes smoke. Come join my holy enterprise.
Let your curses stoke the flames. Let your pauper's breath purge all
heresy.

Lazarillo de Tormes as a Dog

Not the *pícaro*, or rogue, of the Spanish novel
but a hound whose ribs pop out like staves
in a broken barrel, round head colonized
by ticks, a tongue flapping like a flounder.
Each day after the stalls go down in the market,
he sniffs the debris, scarfing a chorizo rind
or a mushy olive until a faster dog takes it away,
so he begs the butcher, who'll give scraps
on a fat Saturday, but will mostly throw
any stone within reach. Even the blind old beggar,
who adopted him as a puppy, drives him out
now that food is harder to buy, beg, or steal
in the dry, hot summertime of Castilla la Vieja.
Lazarillo yowls, whines, slobbers his master's
leprous legs, who curses him like a Marrano Jew,
swinging his cane hurly-burly, then topples
in a rage. For forty days Lazarillo wanders
the crippled scrub, survives on grubs, spiders, moths.
When hunger begins to wring his insides,
he sees a pack of dogs tearing into a squat tree.
None snarl but make way so he too can chomp
its thick hide, chew fatty phloem, wolf down figs
of flesh till it goes bare. Gnawing on bony twigs
they leave for home, a narrow gulch of thistles
by a sandy creek. They work together to hunt hares
or filch carrion from the birds, and their range
extends as the pack learns to trap lambs
in the steep hillsides or catch the bony fish
that float dead when they piss in a slow creek.
Villagers pursue with slaughter on their minds.
Many die, beheaded, quartered, burned to ash
in bonfires, without lull, truce, or charity
of any kind. But the pack is tenacious, conniving,
or just lucky, and Lazarillo, inveterate survivor,
leads them in ambush, nightly raids, daylight forays,
holding ground fast around the squat tree.

Philip II of Spain

Abstemious gourmand, pious hoarder
of martyrs' bones and chiaroscuro saints,
priggish horseman, an emperor brought low
when his Invincible Armada suffered
first a freak storm then got bombed and burned
by Elizabeth's ragtag men-of-war.

He found solace as builder of the Escorial,
his palatial monastery on the iron slag
of ancient mines, Sierra de Guadarrama,
praised by poets as the eighth wonder,
he the Second Solomon, executed
with pulley and garrote, rack wheel and barrow,
Indian miners dying by the thousands
in the silver veins of Potosí, high Andes,
the ingots collateral for loans to raise
not just stone but to wage holy war on heresy
in an empire where the sun never sets.

As debts mounted, rebellion spread, alliances frayed,
the aged monarch retreating to his palace,
its gridiron plan in honor of martyred St. Lawrence.
Racked by gout and dropsy, he limped among
the granite Kings of Judah, his Jerusalem
thorns in bloom, the setting sun a leaden doubloon,
dreaming an Armada to crowd the horizon—
reliquaries with crucifix masts, hair-shirt sails,
and marrowbone canons, racing in wakes
of blood toward the Protestant Gravelines.

Milagro

for Hart Crane

So banal to die on land (continent or lone
Atoll), to expire in flight no tragic fate,
Just hard luck, but to drown in a cyclone
Frees the soul to abandon its bone crate
And mambo to doomsday on gales of grace,
Wiggle to the beat of billows' conga tract.
When the mako or great white gives chase,
A castaway does not linger long intact
In its jaw of saws, gastric juices that burn
Through bone. Any residue will churn
To a cure in the acetic swells of a tempest,
And if salt with heat collude to revive skin,
Cartilage too, the aquiline nose gets blest
As a squid that snorts jets, sneezes poison
On tidal prey. A child's ear might snatch
A reef, then calcify—a charm—among spores
Of madrepore; or a cystitic bladder catch
The Easter gale with ease, but if cast ashore
On the hottest day squish to a jellied flow.
Imagine Loyola lost at sea. He'd sigh *milagro*
To touch sargasso and feel the sharp tingle
Of His thorns, hear death's gurgle, sniff
Those bilious tears. He'd pray for tropical
Inclemency, if not a cyclone at least a stiff
Gale, his sole devotion to drown in a storm,
But the stubborn calm enrages the Basque
Saint whose rowboat drifts too near a warm
Cove. Loyola panics, dives the shallows, a cask
Of silt, then fast currents drag him to black
Sands, a quick mummy in binds of sea wrack.

Nine Benedictions for the Middle Ages

Holy
your candles
of tibiae

Holy
your rosaries
of carious teeth

Holy
your cornucopia
of crania

Holy
your rickets
of Pentecost

Holy
your angels
of gout

Holy
your scapulars
of scapulae

Holy
your schisms
of sinew

Holy
your caritas
of tendon

Holy
your alms
of marrow

St. Cecilia of the Andes, Patroness of Musical Butchers

after César Vallejo

Heavy hoofs drumming the mountain, old bulls file
in procession to St. Cecilia's gambrel cross, her chapel
a belling abattoir, blood mortaring stone, a rawhide roof
strained taut, rain's tambourine, cold winds that clack

her chime of hocks like castanets. At the altar block,
ewes' bells ring canticles, caged hens cluck the metronome,
and St. Cecilia, trilling Ave Maria, saws a cow's shank,
strokes down-bow, up-bow until bone cracks, spiccato.

Rock doves coo, tallow candles glow, and Mass begins.
Quechua girls, acolytes, strum the Kyrie on rib-cage harps.
Cecilia hones steel on Inca stone, cleaves the paschal
lamb from a singletree. Mallets of femur, vellum-tipped,

twin girls duet on a spinal xylophone, arpeggios of Gloria
in Excelsis, while the saint trims suet, twines innards,
plucks warm sweetbread, chops the cleft heart, staccato,
gives fatty alms to hounds baying at the rood screen.

Bladders blare Benedictus when twelve *pauluchas* gather
for the Eucharist, boys who hum, squeak like alpacas,
wear whole animals' skins, two-toed clogs, ear tassels
of scapular, brass crosses that clang around the neck.

Whistling Agnus Dei, St. Cecilia and her acolytes mince
in duple time, serve the feast in clay patens, each morsel
sacramental as she bows before the sun, drinks blood
with snow. The Mass over, *pauluchas* nap until vespers

when she herds them up the glacier to fight with butts,
kicks, stones. Victors raise flags, build barrows, chorus dirges.
As the wounded shiver, St. Cecilia cuts into livers and hearts,
sings a *huayno* to summon heaven's condor, Apu Kuntur.

Day of the Condor

after a photograph by Sebastião Salgado

The ground straw and chaff, hackled scrub, scree of clouds.
Father and son wear paisley crests, conical, red-scarf wattles,

small racket wings of feathered fabric. Arms aloft, wind-
tilted, they pose for the Nikon, its eye refractive, hyperfocal,

to prey in wide angles, panoramic shots. The boy plays cute,
tongue peeking, the father's legs taut, talon-toed in rarified air,

his stare hard, jagged, raptorial, amusing the photographer,
quick to see lucre, the native's glare so prized by buyers.

Nikon blinks, photons strike retinal crystals, silver bromide.
He cans the spent roll, shakes hands too fast, pressed for time,

many more to shoot, and pets the flapping boy, throws him
gumballs to chase across stones. Takes off in a pickup truck

waiting downhill. His bag rattles with the day's hunt, souls caged
in celluloid to bathe, embalm, and fix taxidermically in a sink.

He will garner accolades, that Louvre commission due by now,
maybe the Prix Nadar, an archival vault in the Guggenheim, his work

exquisite to eyes that ply the mausolea of marbled boulevards.
Their request for a ride home ignored, father and son walk down

the shepherds' trail, cull condors' calcite quills, speckled eggshells.
Lambs leap ravines of jasper dust as they chat about the gringo

who swore he'd save their souls in glass shrines seen by thousands,
a story to tell around the stove or by a wake's candle, how they flew

through quicksilver clouds, diamonds' hail, roosted with condors
when they molted to angels, mourned the falling sun, sang the new moon.

Wreath of Desert Lilies

road to Jorge Chávez International Airport, Lima, 1980s

Jets etch lead skies, diesels drone, smokestacks spew dust
That palls pickers' huts, scrapped tin, thatch of broken brooms.
Boys dig up balls, girls cull dolls to mend. Down flumes
Of debris, household scrub, they shoot gulls, slings that gust
Round stones. The mother harrows by tar ponds, rust
Swales, and thinks of home, its rich soil, ice lakes, coca blooms.
War made her flee to these dunes where hunger looms
Despite hard work or faith, but still she prays to Mary's bust
For rains that never come, just winter's metallic mist,
Nor does Christ return, so old tires bake to wheels of bread.
Those rare times Lenten light can pierce the steel haze,
Her spirits improve, joints don't ache, and she'll wrest
Open the white box beneath a rebar cross, its small bed
Of rubber roses, and hold shoes, clothes, locks soft as maize
                             Silk, first daughter's, born in May's
Calcareous light, the happy child who taunted death
With a weak heart. At age six when she drew her last breath
                             The mother braided a wreath,
Desert lilies, but kept it, hung from a cross, to recall
Daughter's grace, soft poise, as she culled the refuse shoal.

Panegyric for Vallejo

As the youngest son, you were destined to wear
the priest's collar, like your Spanish grandfathers—
instead you grew up *el poeta*, rhymes ascetic,
hair shirt of tropes knotted in *barroco* weaves,
your muse Jesús nailed above the cramped desk.
Though you later married, witnessed war, took up
the workers' cause, you lived poor as a friar,
odd jobs, a bit of charity to sustain your calling.
Agony was sulfur to your fire, sadness distilled your verse,
and guilt the lingering aftertaste when you left
a churlish poem to die or lashed at your wife
for buying a new dress. You spent your last years
in Paris, a stale hotel room with garlands
of spider web, your leather books pawned for bread,
Georgette scrimping on potatoes in winter
for bundled paper, ink jugs, a pen that never leaks.

Melville in Lima

My birthplace, you wrote, *strangest, saddest city thou canst see.*
Why such gloom? Because we have no rain, thus *tearless*,
no sun at all in winter? Murky skies lift our spirits.
The cold ocean mist, *garúa*, that mildews convent walls
is our faith's patina. Those *crosses all adroop* serve us well
to hang scapulars big as flags. When buzzards roost
on rooftops, we see Dominicans, tonsured and aquiline,
wings clasped in penance. We sing doxologies to virgins,
prowl the shore in case martyrs' bones wash up. You
call us idol mongers, tawdry in prayer, lazy with scripture,
our *churches more plentiful than billiard tables*. If Mother Spain
is *a great whale stranded on the shores of Europe*, are we
its grotesque calf, unsuckled, left to dry in the neap tides
of superstition? We are Latins, not yeoman yanquis.
Those plain churches in your cherished Chesapeake Bay
are mere hovels to us. We prefer overwrought façades,
garish bell towers, rituals rich with condiment. Gilded altars
rouse our faith, candles titillate, incense makes us
so giddy we can crawl on cobbles as if plush pillows.

Marina

To fend off Lima's *rateros*—ratty thieves—
houses had armored windows, high walls
spiked with broken bottles, my neighborhood
cinema a redoubt of chain-mail drapes,
barbed-wire festoons where I could safely watch
Bambi and *Pinocchio* with Marina, my maid
from Pomabamba, a childless widow,
thick, rooty legs, belly like a sandbag,
her black braid majestic as a mare's tail
at a military parade when she'd trot in brogues,
swing that baton of vulcanized rubber
to beat beggars, hawkers, con men, a bottle
of alcohol inside her purse in case a shoeshine boy
touched my arm, this city full of bad men,
she'd say, where a street clown can be a kidnapper,
candy seller a cannibal, so she'd bribe
the cinema's usher to let us go behind the screen
and up a spiral stairwell to the roof,
a cement incline, parapets of cinder block and rebar,
where we hopped the cowls, took turns
playing goalie and kicker, unleashed marbles
bouncing like hail, chuckled to think we'd startled
moviegoers off their seats, but one Sunday
we heard the temblor of bells, Church of the Nazarenes
a fogless day that winter, the third year
of plagues, hundreds dead in shantytowns,
while down below a minivan cortege
rattled *huaynos* on a megaphone
as it lurched toward St. Christopher's Hill,
a warren of shacks, tinplate niches
that spilled over like debris in a mudslide,
then Marina's hand shackled my wrist
as she cried for her husband, nine years dead,
swore she loved me as her own son,
that she'd give up her life to save mine,
and from then on checked my shoes

each morning for scorpions, smelled my breath,
poked my stool for omens, set votive candles
around my room at bedtime, scattering mothballs,
booby traps, she'd call them, as she prayed
the rosary in Quechua, kept vigil through the night,
my wrists chained to crosses, copper bells.

Angel

Lima, 1968

Rumors adrift of coup d'etat, communist rule,
Mamá sure that our recent guest, a fireball
Furtive by day, night's murmurous ghoul,
Augured the kind of calamity no wall
Of novenas can stop. She hired a shaman
To fumigate, strew charms, lay traps of holy oil—
No respite, omen invasive, her mind a din
Of fears that fracture then form again to roil.
October, the junta's tanks rolled to martial
Law, decrees to collectivize, expropriate, expel
The foreign rich. We fled to Miami, our exile
Of rage in the sun, her portent now the angel
That mocks her grief in nightmares, vowing a slew
Of ills, God's silence, dread fears tolling true.

St. Martin of Porres, Apostle to the Poor

I have lived in your shacks of straw & mud, drunk from your brown creeks, climbed your bald foothills of charity, I the orphaned mulatto born in a donkey's trough, weaned on straw & chaff. I grew up the beggar of seeds, almsgiver to strays, then was by chance apprenticed to a barber but bungled combing, inept at leeching, loose with razors. So I joined the Dominicans, a lay sweeper, my skin too dark for holy orders, hair too nappy for the abbot's hot iron. Misfortune was my blessing. How else could I have become your Bishop of Brooms, my crosier that sweeps away the sins of the world, my miter the do-rag I wear to scrub naves. Jesus favors the lowly laborer, bruised of knee, rickety boned. The rich are wrong to think they will go to Heaven. Their gold offerings evaporate to dross, their pleas drain like water through limestone. Give thanks to Our Lord for linty purses, empty cupboards, calloused soles.

St. Rose Counsels the Washerwomen of Lima

Cast off those husbands at the tavern, drag those kids to the
foundling house, & come live in my convent of cleanliness,
sisterhood of thorned habits, thistle sandals, rawhide girdles. Silent
toil will be your rule as you stoke the copper vats, starch wimples
to discipline. Bleach will smother like honey your pruned-up hands.
Your bare knuckles will rasp washboard Te Deums. Want to be
the Bride of Christ? Pain alone can lure his love. The cloistered
coquette learns to flirt by flagellation, wears a goat-hair negligee,
primps with quicklime, red pepper. She distrusts spectacles, demands
caustic benedictions. She has no need of priests in gilded chasubles
or altar boys dancing with silver crowns. Holy is her laundry water
at workday's end, her chapel sooted & clotheslined, her soap
sacramental, lye from Lenten ash.

St. Anthony and the Sow

One sunny Good Friday, inside a laundry
trough by the outhouse, a sow births cherubs
with kinky tails, clubbed feet, fatback wings.
Despite laboring zealously, the pig dies
without reward. Animals cannot be canonized.

Though in porcine years older than Sarah
when she had Isaac, she's no scrawny beast
but a quarter-ton, razor-tusked, albino hog,
glaucomic rooter of graves, whose final grunt
startles a barefoot nun beating wet wimples
on a stone. She shouts, leaps, cartwheels.
Lay washerwomen kneel before the martyr,
wrap the stillborns in tobacco to be smoked
back to heaven, bathe the live ones in seawater.

Altar boys storm the convent with axes,
keen to chop the sow into a dugout,
row across eddies, raid the convent's groves.
The nuns fight back with paddles,
vats of lye, yet the boys, covered in pigskin,
continue their assault. Right then,
St. Anthony, who'd come to pick up albs,
breaks up the fight, beats heads
with a fat figwood crutch, and the boys flee
toward tabernacles of bamboo.

His crutch striking the ground, he orders
one nun to light the cherubs rolled into cigars,
another to fan the flames, and after saying
a prayer, St. Anthony harvests the sow's fat
for unctions, christenings, exorcisms, etc.,
promises God to raise the survivors, who grow

obese, clumsy, rude, crapping on rivals' food,
hoarding theirs, pewter bells tight on jowls
as they trample through the town streets, eager
for the swill that falls from windows,
grunting in the hail of pits, cores, and rinds.

Acolytes

1

Toward the Yucatán, their island tapers
like a caiman's snout into deep-water gyres,
and though rain seeps into friable limestone, squalls rip
any fruit tree that gets marooned to shore,
even the strangler fig clawing the gray rocks
on a tidal ridge. The acolytes' bamboo huts split
like chicken bones, wells turn saline, porcelain shrines
crumble to coquina along the breakwater.

2

After a squall, dawn's light sparkles like sugar
along guava horizons. Soft waves break
to meringue, scatter seeds of Calvary, stigmatic scrub
that acolytes chop for altar fires or fuel to bake
Lent's red-clay crucifix. They sleep naked in jute
hammocks, surf-side barracoons, then wake
to crows' carillon, bathe in bilge, eat salty gruel,
heads bumped by coconuts dropped from a tolling tree.

3

Long days are spent cleaning the coral cathedral,
ironing cassocks, polishing pyxes, knitting cilices.
Supper is boiled whelk, fronds, jellyfish flan,
though on Easter Sunday clouds of molasses rain rum
into their gaping mouths. Catechism requires
kneeling on coarse sand, stones in outstretched hands,
any moaning punished with cod-oil purges,
priests who whip while singing the Benedictus.

4

Most obey out of terror, of course, but what about
the peewee acolyte, the class clown, the brunt
of jokes, who skips Mass on a sunny spring Sunday
while others drudge at the altar, spends his time
chasing gulls, popping jellyfish, blowing gills like kazoos, etc.,

yet he soon gets that itch of boredom, and since
going back would mean having to do three hundred pull-ups
on a spiny cross, he decides to run away in a shallop.

5
The truant rows hard past the waifs of sand,
sunken caravels, toward a cormorants' rookery
where he scuttles the boat, dreaming of his
own kingdom among the birds. He stakes an oar
in the graveled shore like some conquistador,
prays the Ave Maria, makes fire with deadwood,
happy to live on eggs, seaweed, and coconut water,
leaping as the sun sets to mango's reddish gold.

Orphans

One hundred years before the drive-through window,
Old Havana's orphanage has a drop-off box
built into a sidewall, a cross between a dumbwaiter
and a lazy Susan, where the mother pulls a fat rope

to crank the turnstile, ringing a raceme
of bells, and the nun on watch carts the deposit
inside a stained-glass cloister—part nursery,
part barn—to be deloused, scrubbed, then swaddled

in jute before suckling time by a wet nurse
(usually a slave) or a nanny goat. When the midday heat
starts to crinkle infant skin, nuns spritz
holy water with aspergilla, fan with Sunday palms;

censers fumigate against cankers and blights.
Always hustling for alms, the abbess takes planters
on a tour of trellised cribs; the creole men poke,
pinch, make down payments on the darkest saplings,

those they'll transplant in run-down barracoons,
domestics who'll work the sculleries, sugar kettles, stables.
The archbishop might get his prize: an octoroon
hermaphrodite he'll christen Ángel, raise it to sing

that eighth-octave C, Holy Week's operetta.
The remaining orphans—*blancos*, wheat-colored *trigueños*—
spurt with daily buddings, aerations, leachings.
The final cull at age seven: those failing to bloom

condemned to desiccate, the luxuriant ones
grouped into furrows of goodness, strength, intelligence,
if necessary improved with grafts and prunings.
At his nursery by the sea, the archbishop cultivates

those choice evergreens, altar boys to delight
his eye during the tedious Eucharist, smell their flowers
when light floods the Lenten nave, touch those
Easter buds before they wilt.

Parable with Caliban

From one fishing village to another,
he hobbles on barnacle bones, cockle toes,
his grouper's mouth a gurgling chasm,
one gilled ear deafened by a ballistic coconut.
Caliban begs for seaweed, stale guppies,
the measly roe that drifts ashore
with the red tide, but one morning,
when a gang of sows and piglets gives him chase,
he strays far inland where the sun cooks
limestone to quicklime and the deepest wells
parch by early June. Thirsty, tired,
Caliban pantomimes for water, and a blond boy
tosses him an earthen jug. After a few chugs,
he shrieks out a chantey, which crescendos
to a briny sneeze. Lugworms squiggle
from gleaming pores. Onlookers climb trees,
tiptoe on oxcarts. A woman yells,
"Let's fry his juicy eyes, boil the brain."
Another says, "Let's puff his bladder
into a balloon and float to the orphan island
where mangoes ripen to solid gold."
A pregnant girl warns, "Isn't he the merman
who sucks the sweet fat out of newborns?"
Cutters wield machetes, toddlers totter
to bite fatty thighs, but Don Aurelio,
landowning cacique, concocts a plan: "Let's chop
him up to fertilize this valley's tired soil.
Merman's meat is richer than fish meal
or guano." Men hone. Caliban sucks air,
puffs into a squid, cannonading stinky ink.
Hurled blades puncture branchial hearts,
ropes tie tentacles, pegs crucify as men
butcher in unison, and though the tiniest
scrap is mulch for the cacique's fields,
after a week there's no sign of fertility.
Don Aurelio orders that scraps be sold

to fishmongers, who find no buyer,
no eater, not even a prowling tomcat.
Pails get dumped over the wharf.
Then by the light of a full moon,
body parts phosphoresce and swash
toward a shallow reef where they'll dart,
dodder, twirl in eddies of salt
and semen, born again as polyps,
larvae, medusae, Caliban's empire
of quill, shell, mother-of-pearl.

Curandera

Outside her thatched hut on stilts,
raucous cockatoos gorge on soursops,
children scoop crayfish in a bog,
and on cays of ash—white mangrove—
charcoal pyres fume the gibbous moon.

Garlic coronas gracing her coral stove,
St. Mary plucks two bulbs, wrist smashes
claws for *caldo*, cure-all turtle soup—
its gall bladder, fermented in tamarind juice,
a marvelous curative for tapeworms,
volvulus, and spring catarrhs. Seven days

with chicken pox, Boy Jesus sweats
from the fever, scratches sores
that swell, itch like gnat bites. St. Mary dabs
his face with gingerroot, calendula,
and lemon balm, spoons warm syrup
from the ancient worry bush, then sponges
him with brewed sage and pickleweed.

In her tabernacle of spices, cocoa cherubs
suckle papaya nectar, wear loincloths
of green tobacco, skin hairy as yuca root.

Caressing his face, kissing his sores,
St. Mary whispers, "Sleep, sleep my son,
let spoons and ladles chime you alleluias.
Angels will sing you coconut carols,
play custard-apple maracas. Moon's breath
will swathe you tonight, and you'll dream
sweetsop kisses, ointments that soothe
like tongues of green iguana."

Priestess Tata Lucumí

My sash is the boa that suns on a river stone big as the belly of Oshún,
Mother of Sweet Waters. I draw libations from her brooks, render
fat from the manatee, carve shrines from boughs that lap on her
banks. My steeples are the pines on her river's shore, my high altar
Irokó—kapok tree—where maroons, dog-chased, hog-tied, suffer the
master's leather from dusk till cocks begin to crow. Safe from soldier's
steel, slave catcher's mastiff, our orishas dwell in dreams, full-bellied
& quick to dance, smoke tobacco, make love in the cane, unlike the
sullen saints who flap adrift in cold air, untethered to Mother Earth,
their penitent fists like pin cushions, scourged backs the bark of trees
after a hurricane. How Oshún giggles when I stroke her brown feet
with a peacock feather, gurgles like the River Yumurí when I call
her Cachita, Yeyé Cari. Her love cradles me like springwater gushed
from rocky ferns, my body swaddled in the black silt of mangroves
drummed by vesper tides.

Our Lady of Regla Church

Havana Bay, Cuba

Pebbled floor, vacant pews,
a sunlit sacristy
where seashells foretell
who dies or falls
in love, a round woman with gout
and a frond wimple
hawks scapulars sewn
from seamstress scraps,
goatskin medals, sisal-and-seed rosaries,
her hairy right leg
with burn scars like dry bark,
long, wet pigtails
that smell of tobacco
cured by the seashore,
who whirls
her roughhewn cane
like Moses
parting the Red Sea,
shouts benedictions
at a penitent
who crawls
from station to station,
a sack of spiny fish
roped to his back,
silt-smeared hands
that dip a font
by the nativity crèche,
frogs croaking, black beetles
afloat in holy water,
and just as rain starts to fall,
a gust sprays saltwater

on Our Lady's glass shrine,
flutters the tapers,
blows the hawker's wares
toward the high altar
where saints' cobwebs trap moths
big as hummingbirds.

Odalia

for Nancy Morejón

Mujer negra from the sea bluffs of Baracoa,
Odalia dreads drought, freak of nature,
she says, ill-born like a two-headed calf, a mute horse,
a dwarf child abandoned among the hutias
and iguanas, but even if Odalia's cowries auger
torrents, or she proffers goat's blood

to orishas, El Niño brings drought every generation—
1998's the worst in sixty years, when fertile
fields desiccate to dust chaff, mud burr,
and little survives besides African yams,
white-fleshed, that Odalia grates for mealy flour,
unleavened bread that petrifies overnight.

Days the tanker trucks make their rounds,
whistled yells of *agua fresca* race through ruinous
streets, and Odalia teeters down ramshackle
stairs to join lines that crawl until sundown,
then plods home on shoes soled with cardboard
and hemp, cans hoisted on a shoulder pole.

Odalia drinks enough to survive, the rest saved
for gods that crave okra, cilantro, ginger,
those pungent fruits that delight Oshún who sleeps
inside a clay jar filled with aguardiente,
Our Lady who dances to the three *batá* drums.

Havana, still showerless into late August,
tankers idle for weeks, no fuel, no parts, neither scuds
nor cloudbursts to soak Oshún's banana bush,
Odalia foraging mangoes that go rancid at the altar,
her last pesos spent on cigars to make amends.

Under a graveyard's ceiba, she divines
from bones that command her to hurl
Our Lady's statue into the sea, burn the altar
to cinders, remake Oshún from living skin.
Odalia and her neighbors pool for a goat
to slaughter at sunrise—the hide scraped,
varnished with honey, raindrops branded
around Oshún's neck, thunderbolts around her belly—
then chorus prayers for *aguaceros*
that strafe zinc roofs, snap decrepit trees,
so relentless they soften limestone to cartilage.

Ghazal for Mango

for Derek Walcott

Ballistic drupe, clan of anarchic Anacardiaceae, kin to cashew, sumac
  with red bobs on its bough.
Leathery leaves, evergreen, pregnant panicles in white, ovoid fruit
  that clumps a sunlit bough.

Won't you rummage my barrow? Slurp sweet-sweet Alphonse. Sniff
  citrusy Nam Doc Mai.
Peel Ruby. Covet coquette Mallika. Elope with Jamaican Julie,
  haughty on her plucked bough.

Red-blushed skin, mole-dappled, pastels of canary yellow with
  cardamom green, a hairy stone.
Wicked apricot smeared in devil's turpentine, warned the English bishop
  beneath his pulpit's bough.

Mango, a corruption of the Portuguese *manga*, sleeve, itself a mangling
  of the Malayalam *māṅṅa*.
Fruit of friars, galleon's fragrant cargo. A Goan Judas would've
  swung from mango's gibbet bough.

I love how the word cavorts in speech. To Indians, the dying geezer is
  a mango about to drop.
In Cuba, *mango filipino* is the town tart, floozy in the shade, her name
  carved on a svelte bough.

Arroz con mango, Mamá would say, when life got mixed up, absurd,
  like exile, love's madness.
How Uncle Manny got rich selling plumbing, just a fool who'd
  monkey up any crooked bough.

Orlando's first memory of Miami is of his grandmother's mango
  tree, scraggly, mushy fruit.
The boy from Lima saw rain for the first time, heard thunder, smelled
  resin on a wet bough.

Cuban Villanelle

Raindrops chatter on the tamarind leaves,
Houses swell with iguanas, and girls gossip
Of Inés taking men to the plantain trees.

A widow with ten kids, she has skin like olives
Brined, jute hair, gaunt eyes, yet her bony hips
Are lithe as twigs on wet tamarind leaves.

Inés works hard rolling plump cigars and sees
No shame in keeping her money or skipping courtship
To sleep with men beneath the plantain trees.

Oxen get sold for gifts, fields die, kids starve. Wives
In rampage flay Inés, crop hair, hot-wax eyes, rip
Her silk messaline as rain soaks the tamarind leaves.

Crouched with booze, the men slobber pleas,
But no remorse can save Inés from wives who tip
The kerosene and set ablaze her plantain trees.

Smoke floods the fields. Bells peal. Inés flees
To church but wives chase with knives, strip
Her down as rain falls on tamarind leaves
And men mope in the ash of plantain trees.

Susanne of Saint-Domingue

Green-eyed octoroon, dancer of pavanes,
aspiring cantatrice, brand-new wife
to Corsican Joachim, a rum smuggler twice her age
who wooed through creole go-betweens
this coquette with brown-sugar curls who turned heads
every afternoon, strolling in truffled gowns.

Their new château, Joachim's wedding gift,
has coralline walls, amber rosettes,
pearl windows, coquina towers tiled with silver dolphins,
the wharf a block away where he commands
from a dais his Congolese stevedores to load a dozen
ships bound for Charleston and New York.

Susanne pets her Papillon on the silk fauteuil,
plays tarot cards and barbacole in her garden
by the sea, sings to the warblers as they flit
from one clamshell feeder to another, yet still
she complains to Joachim, "I'm bored like a nun."

One Friday morning in July, flustered Susanne
decides to have more fun, so she and her friends
get drunk by dunking into a rum barrel,
then snort licorice snuff, put on papier-mâché masks
to tell racy secrets, dance with phallic gods,

ten stevedores disguised as Pan, around the grotto
of mermaids with the Triton fountain.
All the while her half-brother Elouard stands
beneath a cotton-silk tree painting the bacchanal
in oleo. Nearby two creole elders—a bishop
and a butcher—peep through the peregrina shrubs,
their hearts palpitating like tambourines.
They shuffle to the grotto with arthritic knees
and demand to join the frolic, threatening to tell
Joachim if she refuses, but Susanna is blunt:

"You're too old, you're too ugly, plus my husband's
deadwood to me." Her stevedores kick out
the elders who mewl like a boatswain's cello.

Soon the bishop makes good on his threat,
and Joachim in a rage ties his stevedores
to a manchineel tree, strips them naked, whips
them in the glaring light, then scores the bark,
its milky sap burning through every cut and sore.
He bribes the governor who sentences Elouard,
ten years hard labor, his sister's head shaved,
her fine garments switched for a sugar sack,
a winding gauntlet of mango stones, patois cusses
as she rides a donkey to the convent on a hill.

Cenobites

for José Lezama Lima

Heaven is bone dust and iodine clouds.
Alluvial marrow, gallstone cays.

Cenobites dredge mangrove catacombs,
then lathe in the sun finger-bone amulets,
scrimshaw doxologies of femur and fibula.

On the leeward side they plow high bluffs—
tartar, calculus—sowing tobacco seeds
that thrive in the urate squalls of Lent.

Cenobites canoe to Santiago's islands—
rocky calvaria—where they cast sisal nets
for fetuses, embryos, even zygotes that escape

Limbo's still waters, and preserved in gourd
reliquaries the unborn sway from rood
trees of black mampoo and Guiana rapanea.

As cherubs spawn in lagoons of rheum
and choirs susurrate litanies beneath a rain
of bile, breakers strew bodies martyred

in fontal seas, every blessèd nose, colon,
kidney, uterus, auricle stewed in conch
pyxes for Easter's callaloo, and in their shrine

of lignum vitae, under a mercuric moon,
the fattened cenobites rumba *la mea culpa.*

Acknowledgments

I am grateful to those journals where these poems first appeared, sometimes in earlier forms and with different titles.

Alaska Quarterly Review: "Ghazal for Mango"
Callallo: "Orphans"
Caribbean Writer: "Acolytes" and "Cuban Villanelle"
Cincinnati Review: "St. Rose Counsels the Washerwomen of Lima"; "St. Dollar Welcomes Cuban Refugees at the Freedom Tower"; and "St. Campesina, Patroness of Water Healers"
Fiddlehead: "Day of the Condor"
Green Mountains Review: "St. Rustica, Patroness of Tobacco Growers"
Harvard Review: "St. Lazarus the African Instructs Those Who Seek His Healing" and "Toussaint L'Ouverture Imprisoned at Fort de Joux"
Hudson Review: "St. Cecilia of the Andes, Patroness of Musical Butchers"
New Laurel Review: "Curandera"
Poetry Salzburg Review: "Philip II of Spain"
Prairie Schooner: "St. Mena, Gardener of Metals"
Sycamore Review: "Odalia"
Third Coast: "Cenobites"

I am especially thankful to Hilda Raz and Elise McHugh for their generous support of this book.

Glossary

agua fresca: Fresh water

aguaceros: Downpours

arroz con mango: Rice cooked with mango

Babalú: A Yoruba orisha (deity) syncretized with St. Lazarus in Cuba

batá: The three cylindrical drums used in Afro-Cuban music

blancos: Whites

bongó: A bongo drum

boogaloo: A type of Latin music

bronco: Rough tobacco

caldo: Clear soup

caramelo: Caramel

curandera: A folk healer (female)

fufu: Mashed plantains (a dish of African origin)

garúa: Cold ocean mist

guasasa: A type of small fly

huayno: A type of Andean dance

loa: A deity in vodun, a syncretic Haitian religion commonly known
    as voodoo

Lucumí: Synonymous with Yoruba in Cuba; the name derives from
    oluku mi (my friend)

Malecón: The sea-wall promenade along Havana Bay

manga: The Portuguese word for sleeve, but also the word for mango

māṅṅa: The Malayalam word for mango; Malayalam is the Dravidian
    language of Kerala in southwest India

mango filipino: Literally a mango from the Philippines, but colloquially
    a loose woman

marabú: The Cuban name of a tree native to Africa

mena: Ore

milagro: Miracle

mujer negra: Black woman

orisha: A deity in *santería*, a syncretic religion of Yoruba origin in
    Cuba

Oshún: The orisha of the river and eros, syncretized with Cuba's
    patron saint, Our Lady of Charity

pauluchas: Boys impersonating llamas in Quechua culture

pícaro: Rogue

el poeta: The poet

ratero: Petty thief; this Spanish word derives from *rata* (rat)

santería: The traditional Yoruba religion as practiced in Cuba

solda: From the Spanish *soldar* (to weld)

el tabaco: Tobacco

tabaco de sal: Salt tobacco

trigueño: Olive-skinned in English, though this Spanish word derives from *trigo* (wheat)

vírgen: Virgin